The Patchsmith's
SPECIAL DAYS MUG RUG

by Amanda Weatherill

PATCHSMITH SPECIAL DAYS MUG RUGS
Text and Pattern copyright © 2014 Amanda Weatherill
Paperback Edition Published: 2020
All rights reserved.

No part of this publication may be reproduced, stored in retrieval system, copied in any form or by any means, electronic, mechanical, photocopying, recording or otherwise transmitted without prior permission in writing from the author.

The designs and projects in this book are copyright but can be made for sale provided they are handmade by the purchaser and credit is given to the Patchsmith for the design. No mass production allowed.

The information given in this book is presented in good faith. The author has made every effort to ensure that the instructions in this book are accurate. Please study the instructions and diagrams for the pattern you wish to make. However, no warranty is given, nor results guaranteed as responsibility cannot be taken for the choice of fabric, tools, human error or personal skill.

CONTENTS

GENERAL INSTRUCTIONS (Fabric, techniques, etc)............1

MUG RUG PATTERNS

HOUSE AND HOME MUG RUG 9

HEART BANNER MUG RUG 13

FLOWER BASKET MUG RUG 17

TUXEDO MUG RUG 21

CELEBRATION CANDLES 25

FLAG HOLIDAYS MUG RUG 29

AFTERNOON TEA MUG RUG 33

PUMPKIN PATCH MUG RUG 37

HOLIDAY WREATH MUG RUG 41

CHRISTMAS TREE MUG RUG 45

About the Patchsmith 50

General Instructions

Before you start

Read through all instructions for the pattern of your choice before beginning any design. The fabric requirements and cutting directions for the design are given at the beginning of each pattern. All seam allowances are ¼" and are included in cutting sizes. You can press seams open or to one side, whichever you prefer.

All the patterns can be used using machine stitching and Celebration Candles mug rug uses a quilt-as-you-go method which is detailed in the pattern. However, if you prefer hand-stitching then I would recommend you choose one of the appliqué patterns – these are suited to hand or machine stitching.

Using the patterns

Read through all instructions for the pattern of your choice before beginning. It will help when choosing fabrics. If your chosen pattern includes appliqué you will find the appliqué templates with the pattern, printed at the exact size. Some of the appliqué images have been reversed – you should trace them exactly as shown and they will be the right way round on your finished mug rug.

Fabric Choices

Due to their size, mug rugs are an excellent use for some of those fabric scraps left over from a bigger project. The appliqué detail uses much smaller pieces – perfect for using scraps, charm squares or recycled fabrics. I just have two requirements from my fabric: firstly, it has to be 100% cotton and secondly, it must be colour-fast. If you stick to these two rules you will be fine.

If you are new to mug rugs or small quilts then a good way to build up a fabric stash is to use pre-cuts i.e. charm packs. These can be found in any fabric shop. It is also handy to have a few fat-quarters (quarter of a yard) ready for background and backing. A good background fabric will have a small print and not be too bold in design or colour.

Do not neglect the backing fabric either. There is a tendency to use fabric that we are not so keen on or do not like, in the belief that it will not be seen. However, if you are gifting a mug rug then use a nice piece of fabric for the back.

Mug rugs are meant to be fun – they give you the opportunity to try new techniques and to play with pattern and colour for very little outlay. So enjoy yourself. As you become more experienced you can try new fabric and colour combinations

Buttons, Ribbon and Trim

Mug rugs are functional mini quilts. Cups and mugs are placed on them along with cookies, cakes and biscuits. Spills and drips are unavoidable and as such, it is important that mug rugs can be laundered.   Ribbons, labels and trims can add an extra dimension to little quilts but make sure they are suitable for laundering and ironing before adding them to your quilt.

It is also important that cups are steady when placed on a mug rug. Buttons seldom cause a cup to topple unless they are particularly large or have a shank. For all patterns in this book you should select only buttons that lie flat (no shank) unless you are intending to hand the mug rug on the wall. However, if you are gifting a mug rug or you are in any doubt, fuse and stitch a circle of fabric/felt in place of the button.

Appliqué

All patterns in this book use the quick and easy fusible method of appliqué. You will need lightweight fusible webbing (i.e. Bondaweb, Vleisofix, Wonderweb or similar). Each pattern includes appliqué instructions but here they are in a little more detail:

1.   Trace around the appliqué shapes onto the paper side of the fusible webbing. Fusible webbing has two sides – one smooth (paper side) and one rough (webbing side). Trace the design onto the smooth paper side.

Hand stitching adds a rustic feature whilst machine stitching blends well.

2.   Cut out the shapes roughly (do not cut out accurately at this stage). You should leave approximately ¼" free around each shape when cutting out.

3.   Follow the manufacturer's instructions to iron the fusible webbing cut outs onto the WRONG side of your chosen fabrics. The rough (webbing) side should be facing the WRONG side of your fabric and you will be ironing the paper side. DO NOT IRON THE WEBBING SIDE – YOU WILL RUIN YOUR IRON.

4.   Allow the fabric to cool completely before cutting out the shapes accurately along the traced lines.

5.   Peel the paper away from the fusible webbing/fabric.

This will leave a layer of glue on the fabric cut outs. Position the fabric cut outs, with the glue side facing down, onto the RIGHT side of the mug rug. Use the appliqué sheet and photo as a guide to their placement and make a note of any pieces which overlap. When happy with the arrangement, fuse the pieces in place according to manufacturer's instructions.

IMPORTANT: *Always leave enough room between the appliqué and the edge of the mug rug to allow for binding.*

6.   Finally stitch the appliqué shapes in position by hand or machine. You can use a running stitch, blanket stitch or any decorative stitch you prefer. It is important to stitch the pieces in place so that they do not come off when the mug rug is laundered.

Quilting

Mug rugs can be quilted with any thick material you have to hand – it doesn't have to be batting or wadding. You can use old towelling, wool fabric, flannel or interfacing. Whatever you use though should be washable and thick enough to protect the table from hot cups/liquid. I use both natural and synthetic materials ranging in thickness from 2 oz to 4 oz.

When it comes to quilting the finished mug rug, you can make it as simple or as complex as you like, whether by machine or by hand. You can even leave the mug rug un-quilted if you wish.

To prepare your mug rug for quilting, lay the backing material with WRONG side facing up, lay the batting on top and finally lay the mug rug with RIGHT side facing up on top of both. (In effect you have a sandwich of batting between the backing material and the mug rug top.) Baste or pin all three layers together, ensuring that the backing and top remain flat and smooth. Quilt as preferred (hand or machine) and quilt around any appliqué shapes.

Tip: The closer your quilting is to the appliqué shape will determine how 'puffed up' the appliqué is. Try stitching very close (almost touching) and then try ⅛" away and see the difference.

 Once all quilting has been completed, trim backing and batting level with the mug rug top.

Binding Methods

There are many different ways to finish your mug rugs. For all the patterns within this book I have used 1¼" wide cotton strips for binding but you could use bias binding if you prefer. I do not cut my binding on the bias unless I want a particular look i.e. a diagonal stripe. All binding is cut from ordinary quilters' cotton fabric.

You can use any binding method you are familiar with or prefer. There are some excellent tutorials on-line for machine and hand binding. I have given instructions here for simple 'single fold' binding and mitred binding.

Single Fold Binding

1. Cut four binding strips each measuring 2" longer than the sides of your mug rug i.e. if your mug rug is 6" x 9" cut two 8" and two 11" strips.

2. With RIGHT sides together stitch a binding strip to the top and bottom of your mug rug. Trim excess binding to match width of mug rug. Press the binding away from the mug rug.

3. Repeat with the two remaining binding strips to the sides of the mug rug. Trim excess binding to match length of mug rug. Press the binding away from the mug rug.

4. Fold the binding round to the back of the rug. Turn under ¼" on the outside edge of the binding and slip stitch the binding in place. Be careful not to stitch through to the front of the rug.

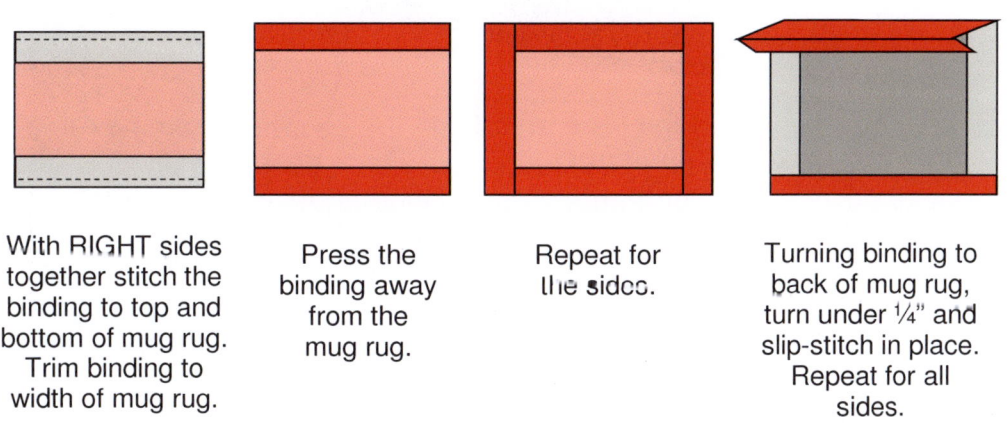

With RIGHT sides together stitch the binding to top and bottom of mug rug. Trim binding to width of mug rug.

Press the binding away from the mug rug.

Repeat for the sides.

Turning binding to back of mug rug, turn under ¼" and slip-stitch in place. Repeat for all sides.

Mitred Binding
This method of binding creates a mitred corner finish for your mug rug.
Note: You will need one continuous length of 1¼" wide binding – this can be constructed from strips sewn together. You will find the length of binding required for each pattern in the Fabric Requirements section at the start of the pattern.

1. Fold the short end of your binding strip into a triangle and align to one edge of the mug rug, RIGHT sides together, as shown (this will create a neat start/finish to your binding). Stitch the binding to the side of your mug rug but stop when you are ½" away from the first corner. Cut the thread and take the rug out of the machine.

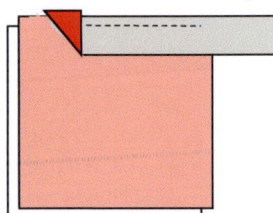

2. Now fold the binding up and away from the mug rug as shown. This will create a triangular fold in the binding at the corner.

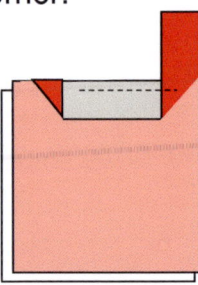

3. Hold the triangular fold (or pin it) before folding the binding down over it, aligning the edge of the binding with the side of the mug rug. Pin to secure in place. Stitch the binding along the side from top to bottom, stopping once again when you are ½" away from the next corner.

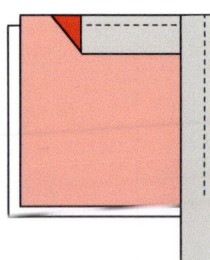

4. Repeat this process for all four corners. Continue stitching the binding until you are 1" past the beginning.

5. Fold binding to the back of the mug rug, turning under ¼" on the raw edge. Slip-stitch in place over the line of machine stitching. Make sure you do not stitch through to the front.

Hanging Corner Triangles

Some mug rugs are so pretty that you may wish to hang one on the wall rather than have it on your table. Or perhaps you already have one on your desk but want to make another. Hanging corner triangles are a great way to achieve this. They enable you to hang a mug rug or small quilt using only one tack in the wall.

All that is needed is two 3" squares of fabric. Fold the squares in half diagonally, with WRONG sides together and press. After quilting and trimming your mug rug and prior to attaching the binding to your mug rug, first pin the triangles to the top corners on the back of your quilt.

Then complete the binding using the method you prefer. As you stitch the binding in place you will also be stitching the triangles in place.

To hang your mug rug all you need to do is insert a pencil or chopstick (trimmed if necessary) into the two corners and hang it on a small tack/nail.

Another simple method to hang small quilts is to attach a small brass ring to the centre top of the back and hang it from this.

So, let us make a start on the patterns.

HOUSE AND HOME MUG RUG
(Finished size: 6" x 8½)

This mini quilt is small enough to sit on a coffee table or desk yet homely enough to add a touch of cosy warmth to any house. You have the option of making this house into a 'home' or adding a country tree addition.

Fabric Requirements:

For the Background: One 4" x 8½" rectangle

For the Side Background: One 2½" x 8½" rectangle *(this can be patched from four 2½" squares)*

For the House: One 6" square for the house
One 4" square for roof
Scraps for chimney, door and windows

For the Tree Sidebar: Three 4" x 3" rectangles
Scrap of brown fabric for trunk

For the Home Sidebar: Four 2½" squares

You will also need:
One 11" x 8" rectangle cotton fabric for backing
One 11" x 8" rectangle of lightweight batting
8" square fusible webbing (i.e. Bondaweb/Wonderweb)
1 yard of 1¼" binding fabric (i.e. bias binding or cotton strip)
Stranded Embroidery Cotton

1. If you are patching the side background, stitch the four 2½" squares together to create a side unit measuring 2½" x 8½" unit. Press.

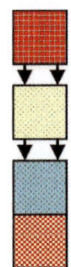

2. Stitch the side unit to the 4" x 8½" background as shown to create a 6" x 8½" mug rug. Press.

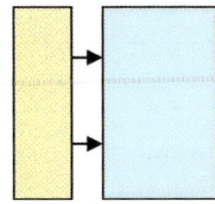

Note: You can add the side unit to either the left or right-hand side of the background rectangle.

3. Trace around all shapes from the appliqué page, onto the paper side of the fusible webbing (Bondaweb). Cut out the shapes roughly leaving approximately ¼" around each shape. Do not cut out along the traced lines at this stage.
Note: The 'home' letters and chimney have been reversed – trace them exactly as shown.

4. Following the manufacturer's instructions iron the fusible webbing cut-outs onto the WRONG side of your chosen fabrics.

5. Allow to cool then cut out the shapes accurately along the traced lines. Remove the paper from each shape.

6. Using the Appliqué Sheet as a guide position the appliqué shapes ensuring each shape is at least ½" away from the edge of the mug rug, with the exception of the tree trunk which should be aligned with the bottom edge of the mug rug. Remember to allow for binding when placing the tree or 'home' letters and place them slightly nearer to the stitched seam than the edge of the mug rug.

7. When happy with the layout, iron to fuse in place. Stitch the appliqué pieces in place by hand or machine.

8. Add any additional stitching.
I added a door knob and house number using two strands of embroidery cotton and a straight stitch. You can add detailing to the windows now or you can quilt it on at step 9.

9. Lay the 11" x 8" backing rectangle, **wrong** side facing up and place the batting on top. Position the mug rug centrally on top with **right** side facing up. Baste or pin all three layers together, ensuring that the backing and top remain flat and smooth. Quilt around all appliqué shapes. Add any further quilting as desired.

10. Once all quilting has been completed, trim backing and batting to the same size as the mug rug top.

11. Bind the mug rug using the binding method of your choice. *(see 'Binding' in General Instructions for examples of binding methods).*

HOUSE AND HOME APPLIQUÉ
Trace around the solid lines
Dashed lines are additional stitching/quilting suggestions.

11

HOUSE AND TREE APPLIQUÉ
Trace around the solid lines
Dashed lines are additional stitching/quilting suggestions.

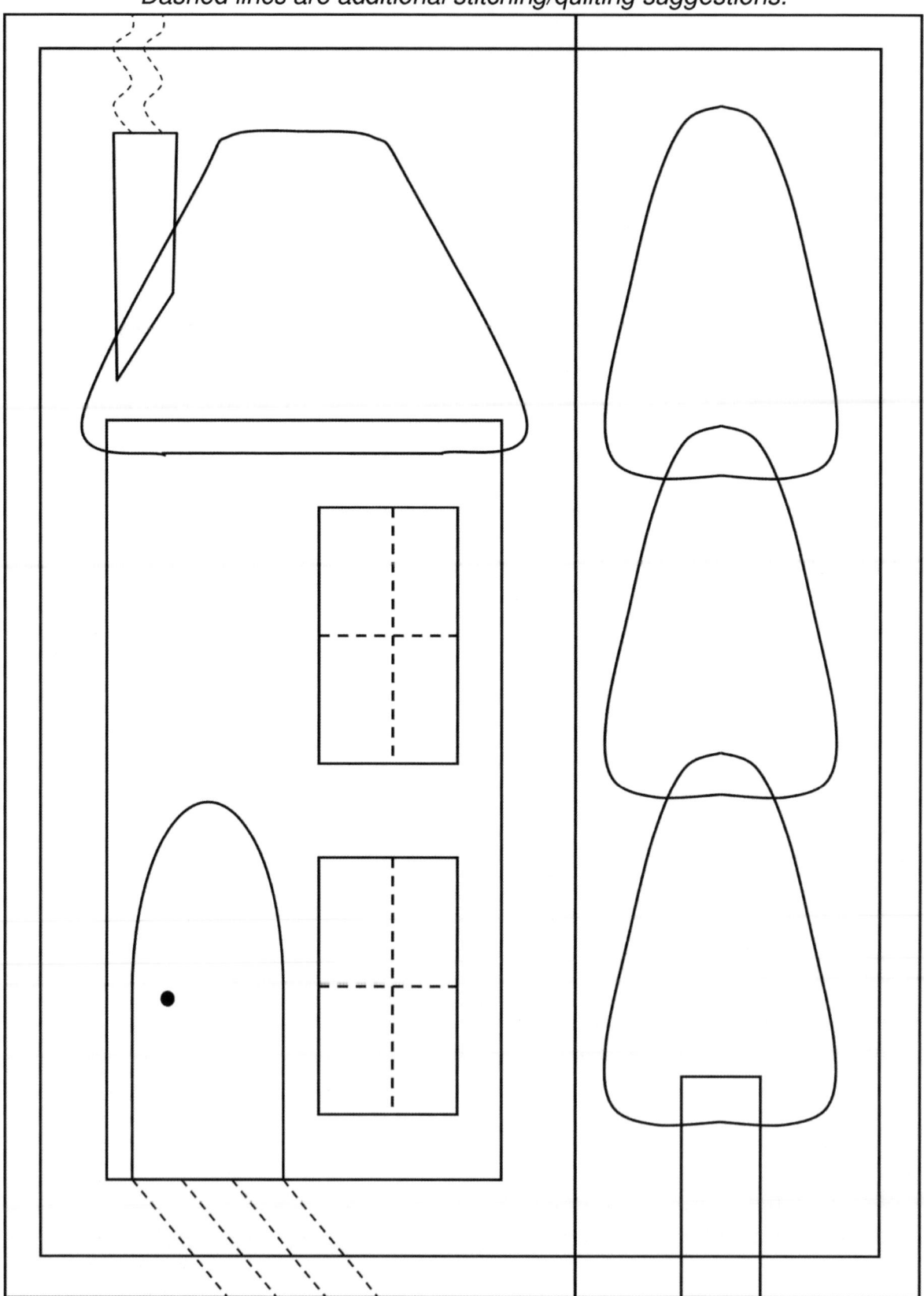

HEART BANNER MUG RUG
(Finished size: 9" x 5½")

Hearts say so much – from love, truth and honesty to homely simplicity
As such this mug rug is well suited to Valentine's Day, as a gift for a loved one or just to reflect your love of mini quilts and mug rugs.

Fabric Requirements:

For the Background:
One 9" x 5½" rectangle

For the Appliqué:
One 5" square for the heart
One 2" x 5" rectangle for the banner
Two 2½" squares for the banner ends

You will also need:
One 6" length of ribbon, string or twine
One flat button or circle of felt
One 8" square of fusible webbing *(i.e. Bondaweb/Wonderweb)*
One 11" x 7" rectangle cotton fabric for backing
One 11" x 7" rectangle of lightweight batting or fusible batting
1 yard of 1¼" of binding (i.e. bias binding or cotton strip)

Mug Rug Construction

1. Trace around all shapes from the page 15, onto the paper side of the fusible webbing (Bondaweb). Trace the three small dotted hearts onto the banner tracing. Cut out the shapes roughly leaving approximately ¼" around each shape.
Note: Do not cut out the dotted hearts at this stage.

2. Following the manufacturer's instructions iron the fusible webbing cut-outs onto the WRONG side of your chosen fabrics.

3. Allow to cool then cut out the shapes accurately along the traced lines. Cut out the dotted hearts from the banner. Carefully remove the paper from each shape taking care not to pull them out of shape.

4. Using the Appliqué Sheet as a guide position the shapes onto the front of the mug rug. The large heart should be positioned first – position it centrally so that the point of the heart is ½"- ¾" from the bottom of the mug rug. The banner lies on top of the heart so that the heart shows through the small heart cut-outs. The banner ends tuck under the banner at either side. All pieces should be at least ½" from the edge of the mug rug to allow for binding.

5. Cut two lengths of ribbon (or twine/string) so that they tuck under the top of each side of the large heart and reach up to the middle of the mug rug as shown.

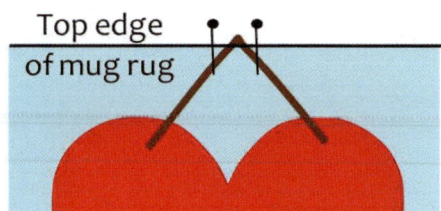

Pin or tack the ribbon in place at very top of the mug rug. You will stitch the ribbon in place when attaching the binding.
Note: *Make sure your ribbon, twine or string can be ironed and laundered.*

6. When happy with the arrangement, iron to fuse all pieces in place, catching the ends of the ribbon under the top of the large heart. Hand or machine stitch around each appliqué shape and around each small heart cut out.

7. Lay the 11" x 7" backing rectangle, **wrong** side facing up and place the batting on top. Position the appliquéd mug rug centrally on top with **right** side facing up. Pin the three layers together, ensuring that the backing and top remain flat and smooth. Quilt around the heart and banner. Add any decorative stitches or quilting as preferred.

8. Once all quilting has been completed, trim backing and batting to the same size as the mug rug top.

9. Bind the mug rug using the binding method of your choice. (see 'Binding' in General Instructions for examples of binding methods). Make sure to catch the ribbon at the centre top of the mug rug as you stitch the binding.

10. Finally sew a large flat button in place at the top of the mug rug. Alternatively, you could use a circle of felt.

HEART BANNER APPLIQUÉ

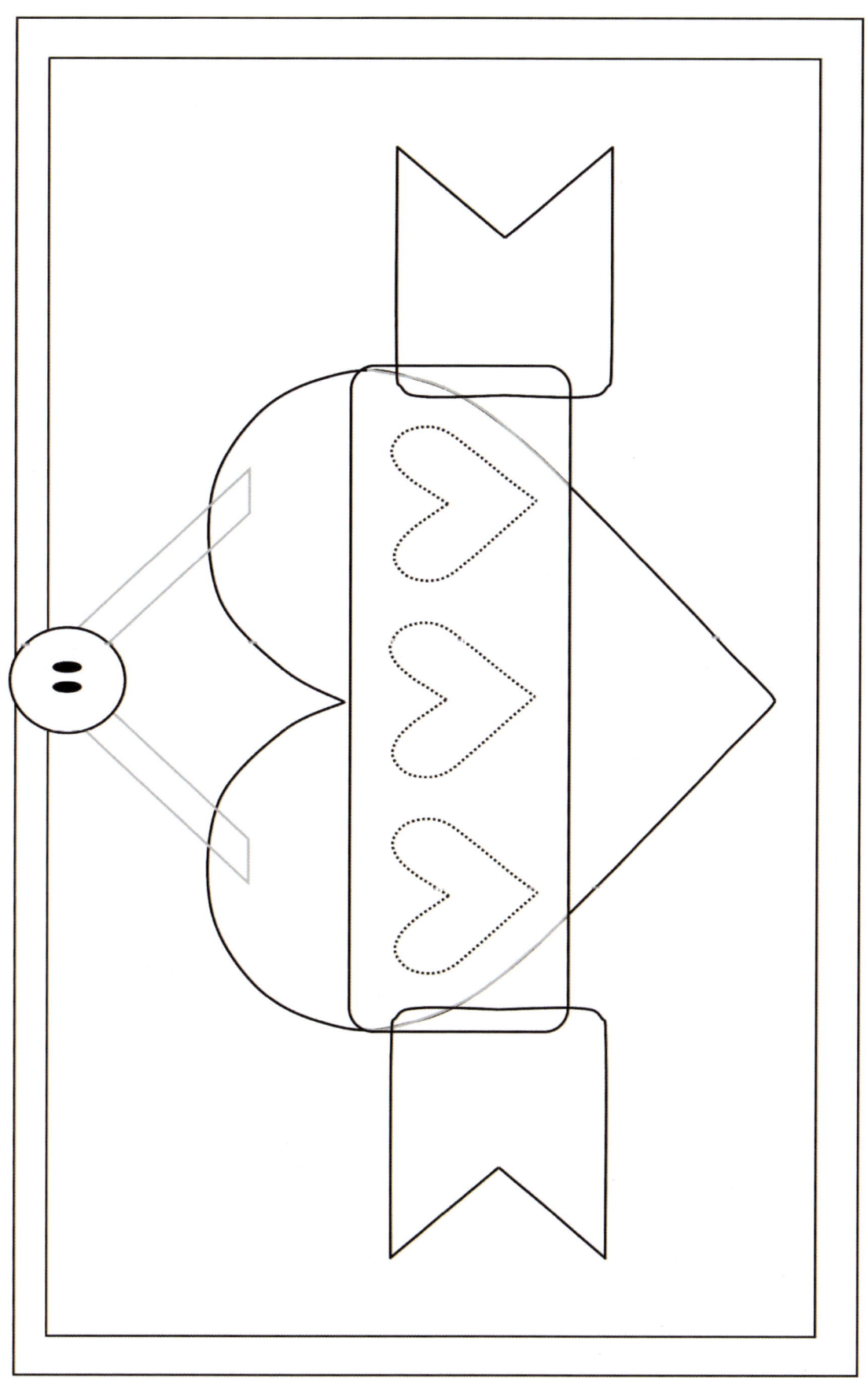

FLOWER BASKET MUG RUG
(Finished size: 9" x 5½")

A basket of flowers is always a delight to receive and this basket is no exception. You have a choice from two designs but whichever design you choose these flowers are sure to last all year long.

Fabric Requirements:

For the Background: One 9" x 5½" rectangle

For the Basket: One 7" x 3" rectangle

For the Large Flowers: Three 2½" squares for petals
Three 1½" squares for middles
One 2" square for the stems

For the Small Flowers: Four 2½" squares for the petals
Four 1½" squares for the middles

You will also need:
One 8" square of fusible webbing *(i.e. Bondaweb/Wonderweb)*
One 11" x 7" rectangle cotton fabric for backing
One 11" x 7" rectangle of lightweight batting or fusible batting
1 yard of 1¼" of binding (i.e. bias binding or cotton strip)

Mug Rug Construction

1. Trace around all shapes from the appliqué page, onto the paper side of the fusible webbing (Bondaweb). Cut out the shapes roughly leaving approximately ¼" around each shape. Do not cut out along the traced lines at this stage.

2. Following the manufacturer's instructions iron the fusible webbing cut-outs onto the WRONG side of your chosen fabrics.

3. Allow to cool then cut out the shapes accurately along the traced lines. Remove the paper from each shape.

4. Using the Appliqué Sheet as a guide and ensuring each shape is at least ½" away from the edge of the mug rug, position the shapes onto the front of the mug rug. Tuck the bottom of the stems under the basket and the tops under the flowers. When happy with the layout, iron to fuse in place.
Tip: If making the Summer Basket version you may find it easier to fuse and stitch the large flowers in place before stitching the flower centres on top. Likewise for the basket.

5. Stitch the appliqué pieces in place by hand or machine.

6. Add any additional stitching if desired.

7. Lay the 11" x 7" backing rectangle, **wrong** side facing up and place the batting on top. Position the mug rug centrally on top with **right** side facing up. Baste or pin all three layers together, ensuring that the backing and top remain flat and smooth. Quilt around all appliqué shapes. Add any further quilting as desired.
I added quilting detail to the basket and tulips as indicated by the dashed lines on the appliqué sheet.

8. Once all quilting has been completed, trim backing and batting to the same size as the mug rug top.

9. Bind the mug rug using the binding method of your choice *(see 'Binding' in General Instructions for examples of binding methods).*
I used a 1¼" wide single-fold binding.

SUMMER BASKET APPLIQUÉ

SPRING BASKET APPLIQUÉ

20

TUXEDO MUG RUG
(Finished size: 9" x 5½")

Good looking and practical – the perfect mug rug for the perfect man in your life – whether that be a relative, friend or even a James Bond fan. This tuxedo comes with its own handy pocket – the ideal place for a gift token, voucher or small gift.

Fabric Requirements:

For the Pocket Background: One 4½" x 5½" rectangle

For the Pocket: Two 5" rectangles

For the Tuxedo: One 2" x 5½" rectangle white fabric
Two 2" x 5½" rectangles black fabric

For the Tuxedo Lapels: One 4" x 6" rectangle grey fabric

For the Tie and Waist sash: One 3" square of contrasting fabric

You will also need:
One 11" x 7" rectangle cotton fabric for backing
One 11" x 7" rectangle of lightweight batting
7" square fusible webbing (i.e. Bondaweb/Wonderweb)
1 yard of 1¼" binding fabric (i.e. bias binding or cotton strip)

Mug Rug Construction

1. With **right** sides together, stitch the black and white rectangles together as shown. Press the seams open. The tuxedo block should measure 5" x 5½":

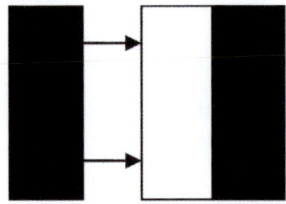

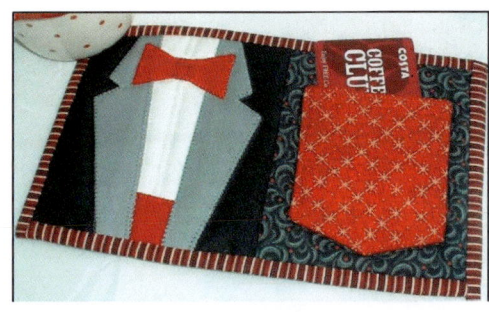

2. Trace the jacket lapels, tie and waist sash from the page 24, onto the paper side of the fusible webbing (Bondaweb). Cut out the shapes roughly leaving approximately ¼" around each shape.

3. Following the manufacturer's instructions iron the fusible webbing cut-outs onto the WRONG side of your chosen fabrics.

4. Allow to cool then cut out the shapes accurately along the traced lines. Remove the paper from each shape.

5. Using the Appliqué Sheet as a guide, position the waist sash centrally along the bottom edge of the block. Place both lapels either side of the middle section of the block so that the lapels cover the seams. When happy with the arrangement, iron to fuse all pieces in place. Hand or machine stitch around each lapel and across the top of the waist sash.

6. Once the lapels are stitched in place appliqué the bow tie. Position the tie so that it is at least ½" from the edge of the block to allow for binding.

7. With right sides together, stitch the tuxedo block to the pocket background to create a mug rug measuring 9" x 5½". Press.

Make the Pocket

8. Cut two pocket pieces from the 5" squares of fabric using the pocket pattern on page 23.
*Tip: The easiest way to do this is to print and cut out the pocket to create a paper pattern. Place the two 5" squares, **right** sides together and pin the paper pattern to the fabrics. Cut around the pattern.*

9. With **right** sides together, stitch the two pocket sections together leaving a 1"-2" opening along one side. Trim the corners and seams before turning the pocket right side out. Turn in ¼" along the side opening and press.
Tip: I used a chopstick to gently push out the corners.

10. Topstitch across the top of the pocket.
I added two lines of topstitching to mimic a real pocket.

11. Place the pocket onto the background square so that the bottom point of the pocket is at least ½" from the bottom edge of the mug rug. Remember to allow for the binding on the right-hand side when placing the pocket (i.e. the pocket should be approx. ¾" from the right edge of the mug rug). When happy with the placement stitch the pocket in position by topstitching down both sides and along the bottom.

12. Lay the 11" x 7" backing rectangle, **wrong** side facing up and place the batting on top. Position the appliquéd mug rug centrally on top with **right** side facing up. Pin the three layers together, ensuring that the backing and top remain flat and smooth. Quilt around the pocket, lapels, tie and across the top of the waist sash. Add two rows of stitching down the centre of the white 'shirt' to imitate the button band. Add any decorative stitches or quilting as preferred.
I added a square of stitching to the centre of the tie.

13. Once all quilting has been completed, trim backing and batting to the same size as the mug rug top.

14. Bind the mug rug using the binding method of your choice. *(see 'Binding' in General Instructions for examples of binding methods).*
I used a single-fold binding.

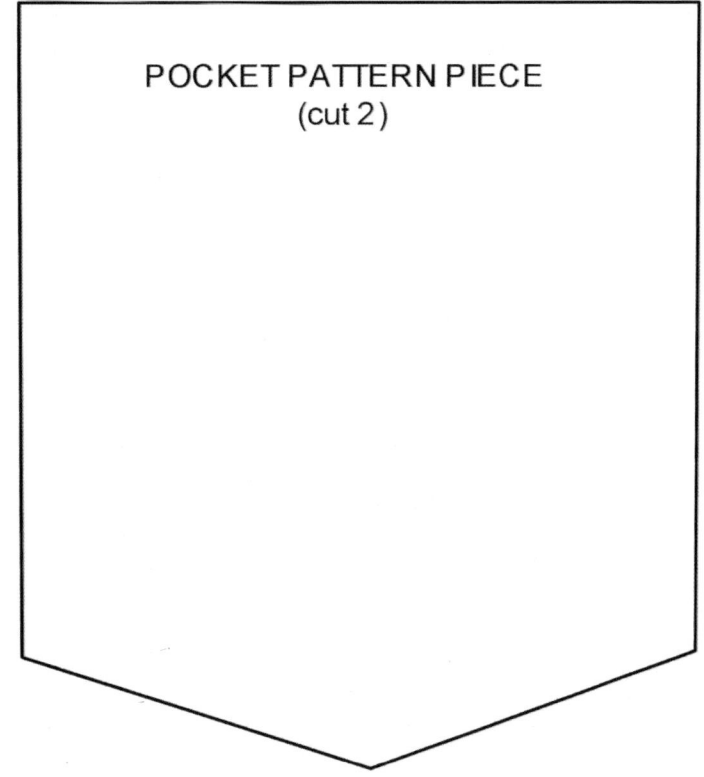

POCKET PATTERN PIECE
(cut 2)

TUXEDO APPLIQUÉ

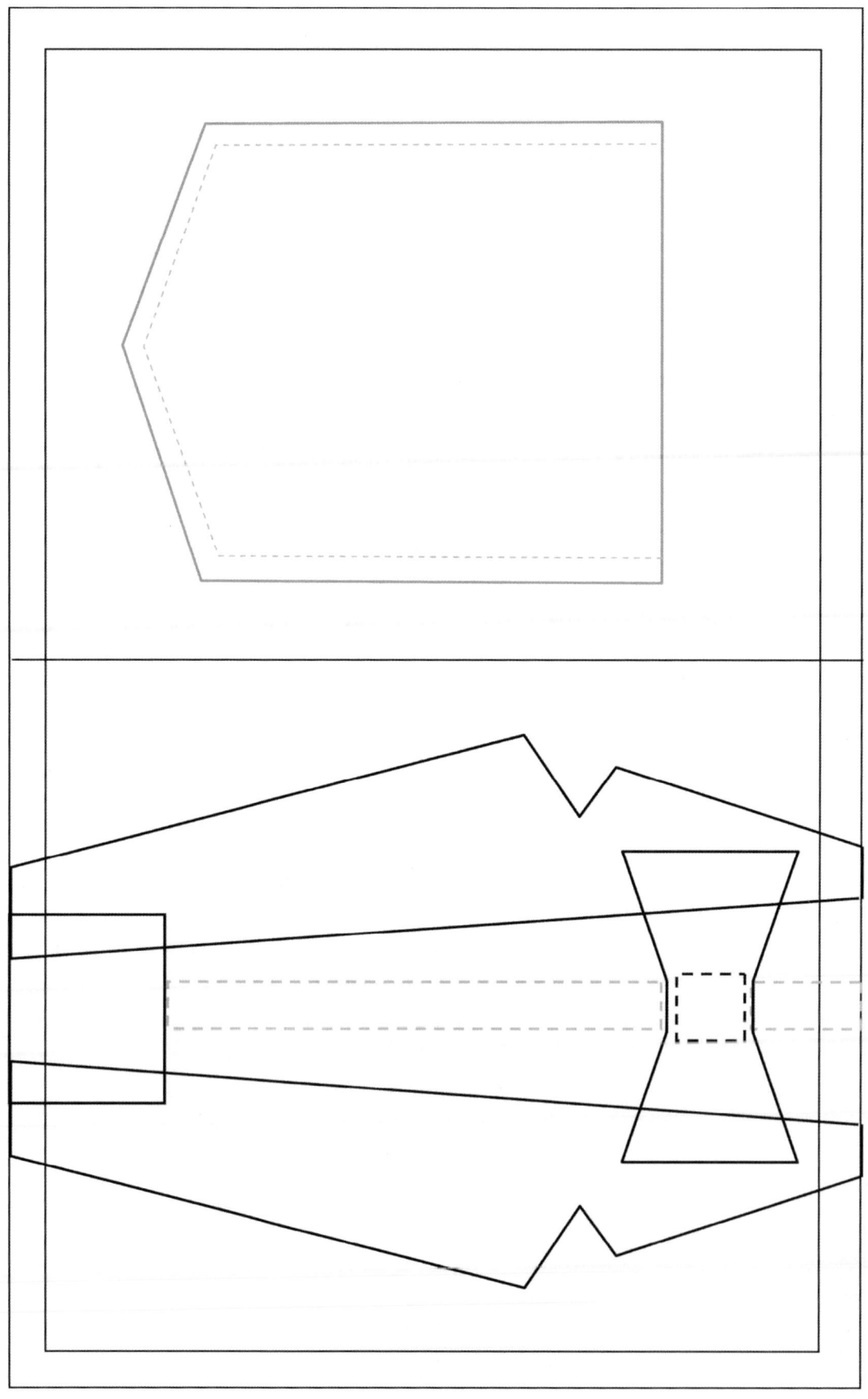

CELEBRATION CANDLES MUG RUG
(Finished size: 9½" x 5½")

No celebration is complete without candles.
With this simple quilt-as-you-do design you can
celebrate with candles every day of the year.

Fabric Requirements:
For the Candles: Nine 4" x 1½" stripes of 'candles' fabric
                     Nine 4" x 1½" stripes of background fabric

You will also need:
One 5" square of yellow/orange fabric for the flames
One 5" square fusible webbing   (i.e. Bondaweb/Wonderweb)
One 11" x 7" rectangle cotton fabric for backing
One 13" x 9" rectangle of lightweight batting
1 yard of 1¼" binding fabric (i.e. bias binding or cotton strip)
Stranded embroidery thread if hand stitching the flames

A note about batting....
*If using synthetic batting you should finger press throughout or use
a very cool iron as some synthetics are not suitable for a hot press.*

Mug Rug Construction

1. With right sides together stitch a background 1½" strip to each 'candle' 1½" strip along the short side as shown. Press seams toward the candle fabric. Each strip should measure 7½" x 1½".

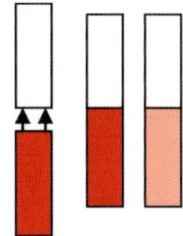

2. Trim three of the candle strips to 5½" long with the candle section measuring 3¾" and the background measuring 1¾" long – see **(A)** below.

Trim three strips to 5½" long with the candle section measuring 3¼" and the background measuring 2¼" long – see **(B)** below.

Trim the last three candle strips to 5½" long with the candle section measuring 2¾" and the background also measuring 2¾" – see **(C)** below.

You should now have nine candle units each measuring 1½" x 5½".

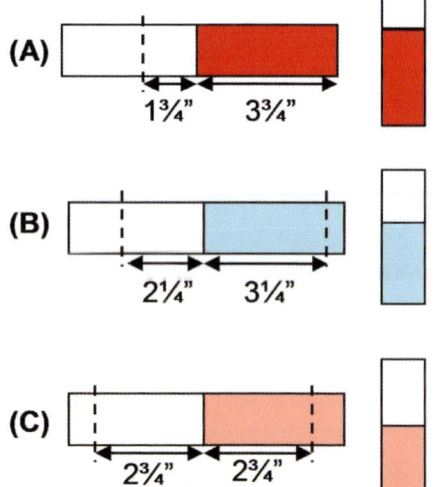

3. Arrange the 5½" strips in the order you wish them to appear on your mug rug top. *Tip: Place different size candles next to each other randomly along the row as shown opposite.*

4. Lay the first candle strip, **right side facing up**, onto the 13" x 9" batting rectangle so that the bottom edge of the candle is 2" up from the bottom of the batting and the left-hand side of the strip is 1" from the left-hand edge of the batting.

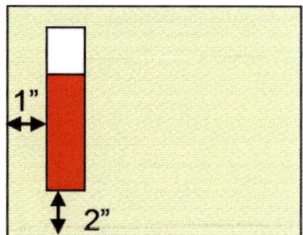

5. Place the next strip, **right side facing down** onto the first strip, lining the strips up exactly. Pin securely in place. Using a ¼" seam allowance stitch along the right-hand edge of the strips, stitching through all layers. Press the two strips open.

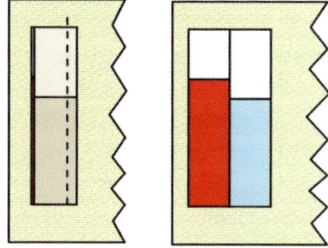

6. Place another strip **right side facing down**, along the right-hand edge of the two stitched strips, pin and stitch as before. Press open. Continue to add the strips in this way until all nine candle strips are stitched onto the batting.

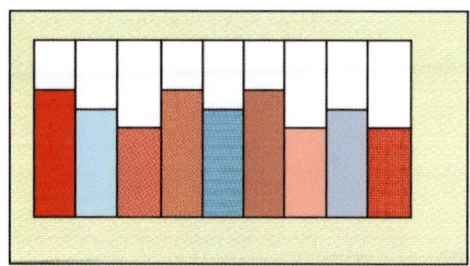

7. Trace around the flame template below nine times onto the paper side of a 5" square of fusible webbing. Cut out the shapes roughly leaving approximately ¼" around each shape. *I used a combination of both flame directions.*

8. Following the manufacturer's instructions iron the fusible webbing cut-outs to the WRONG side of a 5" square of yellow fabric.
Tip: *If you have used a dark background and you think this may show through the flames you could use felt or fuse two squares of yellow fabric together and treat as one.*

9. Allow to cool before cutting out each flame accurately along the traced lines. Carefully remove the backing paper and position the flames onto the quilted candle patch so that there is a gap of ⅛"-¼" between the candle and the flame as shown in the photo below.

10. When happy with the placement, fuse and stitch the flames in place by hand or machine. This will also quilt the shapes in place at the same.

11. Create a wick by stitching from the top of each candle onto the bottom of each flame. If you are machine stitching sew three or four rows very close to each other for each wick. If hand-stitching the easiest way to create a wick is to use two strands of embroidery cotton and a simple long stitch. I used two long stitches per wick.

12. Once all flames have been stitched trim the batting to 11" x 7".

13. Lay the 11" x 7" backing rectangle, **wrong** side facing up and place the quilted mug rug centrally on top with **right** side facing up. Pin or tack the two together securely before trimming the backing and batting to the same size as the mug rug top. Trim the mug rug top if needed but try to ensure the candles remain as straight as possible.

14. Bind the mug rug using the binding method of your choice *(see 'Binding' in General Instructions for examples of binding methods).*
I used a 1¼" wide single-fold binding.

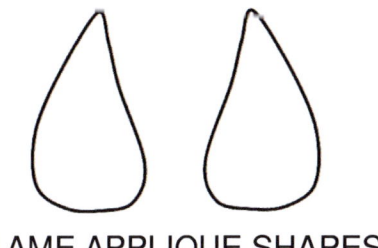

FLAME APPLIQUE SHAPES

FLAG HOLIDAY MUG RUG
(Finished mug rug size: 9½" x 5½")

Every country around the world has a national holiday.
This versatile little mug rug is the perfect table decoration for such a day.
The pinwheel can be made in any colour combination to reflect
the colours of your country's flag.

Fabric Requirements:

Pinwheel Background:	Four 1¾" x 3" rectangles
	Two 2½" squares
Blades (Blue):	Four 2½" squares
Centre (Red):	Two 2½" squares
Star Background:	4½" x 5½" block
Large Star:	5" square
Small Star:	3" square

You will also need:
One rectangle 11" x 8" cotton fabric for backing
One rectangle 11" x 8" of lightweight batting
One 8" square of fusible webbing for appliqué (i.e. Bondaweb)
1 yard of 1¼" binding fabric (i.e. bias binding or cotton strip)

(*See page 30 for fabric requirements if appliquéing the pinwheel*)

Mug Rug Construction

You have a choice of patching the pinwheel block or appliquéing it. Follow the directions below for your chosen method.

Patched Pinwheel

1. Draw a diagonal line on the WRONG side of the two background 2½" squares and the two red 2½" squares - this pencil mark will be your cutting line.

2. With RIGHT sides together lay a marked square on top of a blue square. Sew a scant ¼" away from both sides of the pencil line as shown. Cut along the pencil mark and press the units open. Repeat to create eight half-triangle units (four white/blue and four red/blue). Trim the units to measure 1¾" square.

3. Stitch one white/blue and one red/blue half-triangle unit together as shown to create a blade unit which measures 1¾" x 3". Press. Repeat to make four blade units.

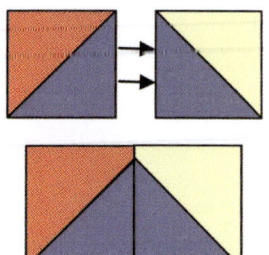

4. Stitch one blade unit to one 1¾" x 3" background rectangle to create a 3" square unit as shown. Press. Repeat to make four units.

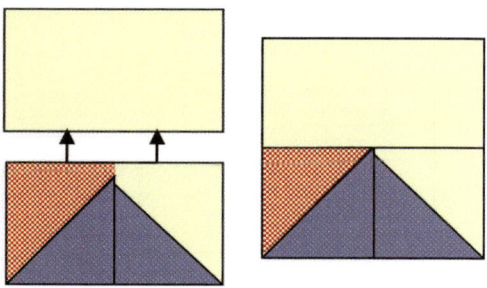

5. Finally, stitch the four squares blocks together to create a 5½" pinwheel block. Press.

Note: You will find it easier to match points if you press the seams open for this step. But don't worry too much – you can always appliqué a small circle of fabric over the centre if you wish.

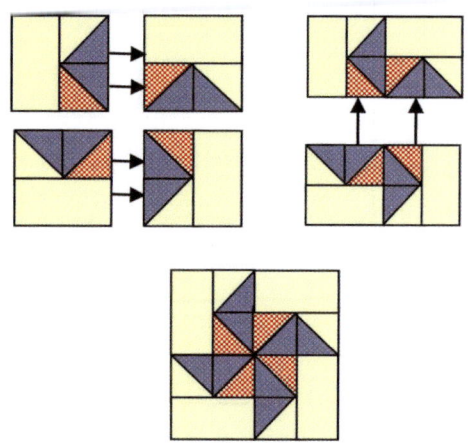

Appliquéd Pinwheel

Fabric Requirements:
- One 5½" background square
- One 3" square for the centre
- Four 2" x 3" rectangles for blades

1. Fold the 5½" background square in quarters diagonally and press lightly to mark the diagonal positions on the background square.

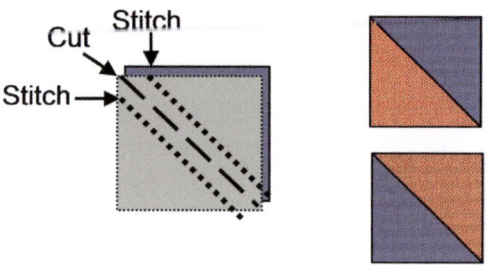

2. Following the instructions given at steps 7-10 below to trace and cut one centre square and four blades from the appliqué sheet. *(Remember to take into account any directional pattern in your fabric choices.)*

3. Position the centre square so that all four corners meet the diagonal pressed lines. Fuse in place.

4. Position each blade so that the point of the blade matches up with a corner of the centre square and all blades meet in the centre
Note: Each blade tip should be just over ¼" from the mug rug edge to allow for the binding.

5. Fuse and stitch the pieces in place.

COMPLETING THE MUG RUG
6. With RIGHT sides together stitch the pinwheel block to the star background to create a mug rug top measuring 9½" x 5½". Press.

7. Trace around the two stars onto the paper side of the fusible webbing (Bondaweb). Cut out the shapes roughly leaving approximately ¼" around each shape. Do not cut out along the traced lines at this stage.

8. Following the manufacturer's instructions iron the fusible webbing cut-outs onto the WRONG side of your chosen fabrics.

9. Allow to cool then cut out the shapes accurately along the traced lines. Remove the paper from each star. Using the Appliqué Sheet as a guide, position the stars onto the mug rug. *Note: The left-hand point of the star should be approximately 3/8" from the centre seam to allow for the binding on the right-hand edge.*

10. When happy with the layout, iron to fuse in place. Stitch the stars in place by hand or machine.

11. Lay the 11" x 8" backing rectangle, **wrong** side facing up and place the batting on top. Position the mug rug centrally on top with **right** side facing up. Baste or pin all three layers together, ensuring that the backing and top remain flat and smooth. Quilt around all appliqué shapes. Add any further quilting as desired.
I shadow quilted around the pinwheel.

12. Once all quilting has been completed, trim the backing and batting to the same size as the mug rug top.

13. Bind the mug rug using the binding method of your choice *(see 'Binding' in General Instructions for examples of binding methods).*
I used a 1¼" wide single fold binding.

Design Suggestion:

Replace the star block with a patchwork block constructed from twelve squares. Cut each square 1¾" x 1¾".

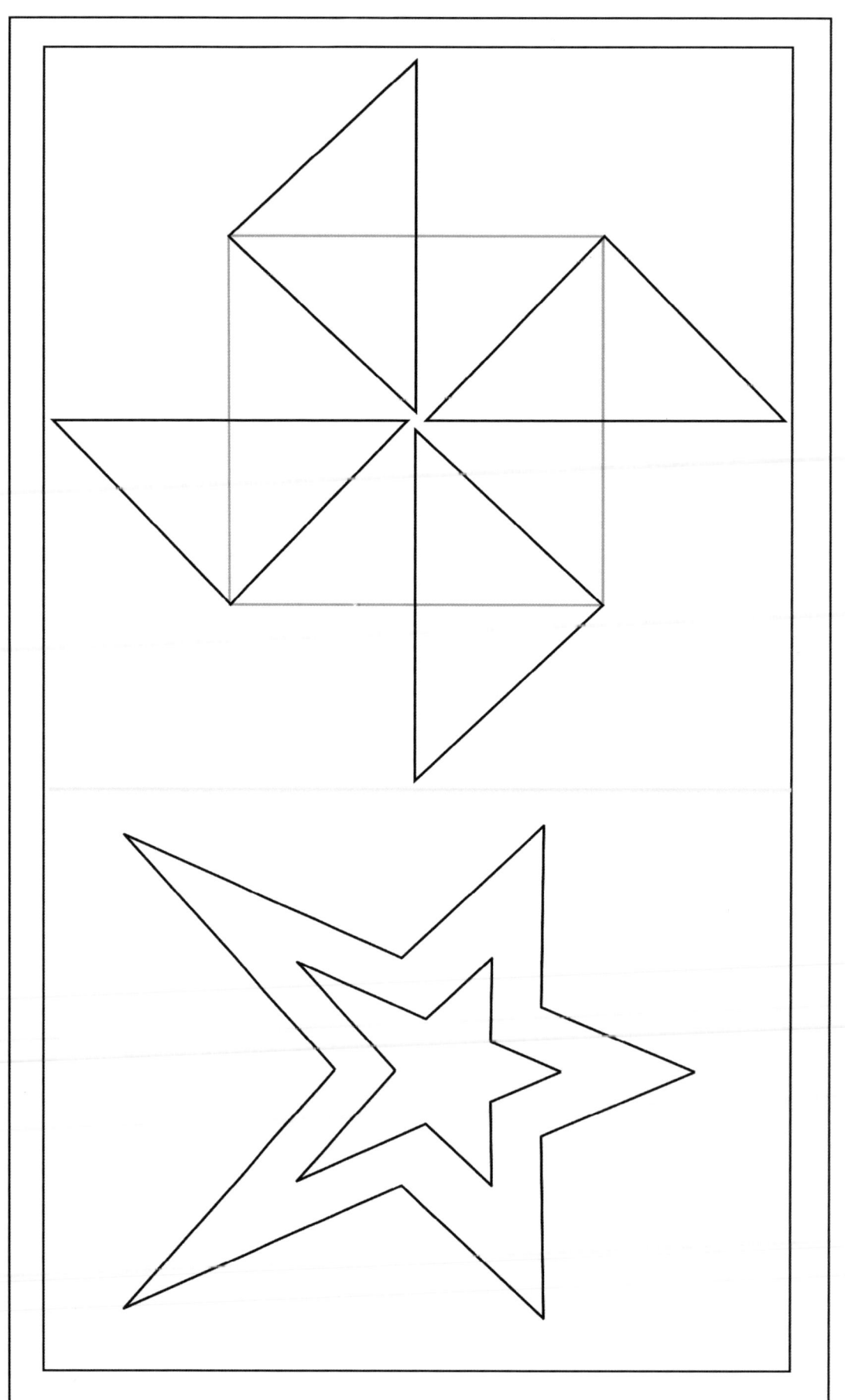

AFTERNOON TEA MUG RUG
(Finished size: 9" x 5½"")

Little finger sandwiches, dainty fairy cakes and lashings of hot English tea.
Afternoon tea is my family's favourite Easter celebration.
But we don't keep it just for Easter – we indulge all through the summer as the large country houses open up their tea rooms to the public.

Fabric Requirements:

For the Background: 9" x 5½" rectangle

For the Cup: One 4" x 1¾" rectangle
Two 4" x 1½" rectangles
One 5" x 2" rectangle for saucer
One 2½" square for handle

For the Cake One 3½" x 2½" rectangle for case
One 4" x 2" rectangle for cake
One 4" x 2 rectangle of felt for icing

You will also need:
One flat red 'cherry' button or circle of red felt (*optional*)
One 11" x 7" rectangle cotton fabric for backing
One 11" x 7" rectangle of lightweight batting
8" square fusible webbing   (i.e. Bondaweb/Wonderweb)
1 yard of 1¼" binding fabric (i.e. bias binding or cotton strip)
Stranded Embroidery Cotton if adding steam spirals

Mug Rug Construction

1. Stitch a 4" x 1½" rectangle to the top and bottom of the 4" x 1¾" rectangle to create a unit measuring 4" x 3¾". Press the seams open.

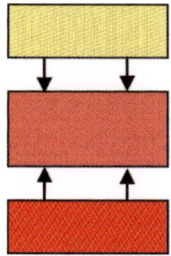

2. Trace around all shapes from the appliqué sheet, onto the paper side of the fusible webbing (Bondaweb). Mark the position of the dotted line on the tea cup tracing. Cut out the shapes roughly - do not cut out accurately at this stage.
Note: The handle has been reversed – trace exactly as shown and it will be the right way round on the finished mug rug.

3. Following the manufacturer's instructions iron the fusible webbing cut-outs onto the WRONG side of your chosen fabrics. You should fuse the tea cup tracing to the WRONG side of the patched rectangle matching the line on the tracing to the top seam on the patched rectangle as shown below.

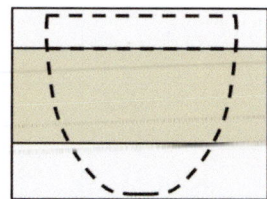

4. Allow to cool then cut out the shapes accurately along the traced lines. Remove the paper from each shape. Using the Appliqué Sheet and photo as a guide and ensuring each shape is at least ½" away from the edge of the mug rug, position each appliqué shape onto the front of the mug rug. The cake lies on top of the cupcake case, whilst the felt icing lies on top of the cake.

5. When happy with the arrangement, iron to fuse in place. Hand or machine stitch around each appliqué shape to secure.

6. Lay the 11" x 7" backing rectangle, **wrong** side facing up and place the batting on top. Position the appliquéd mug rug centrally on top with **right** side facing up. Pin the three layers together, ensuring that the backing and top remain flat and smooth. Quilt around the cup-and-saucer and the cupcake. Add any decorative stitches or quilting as preferred.
I added quilting detail to the saucer, quilted along the seams of the tea cup and hand quilted steam spirals above the cup using two strands of embroidery cotton.

7. Add a flat red button or red felt circle to the top of the cupcake if desired.
Note: *NEVER use a large button or a shank button on a mug rug as it may cause a cup to wobble. If you are in any doubt substitute felt for the button.*

8. Once all quilting has been completed, trim backing and batting to the same size as the mug rug top.

9. Bind the mug rug using the binding method of your choice *(see 'Binding' in General Instructions for examples of binding methods).*
I used a 1¼" wide single-fold binding.

TEA AND CAKE APPLIQUÉ

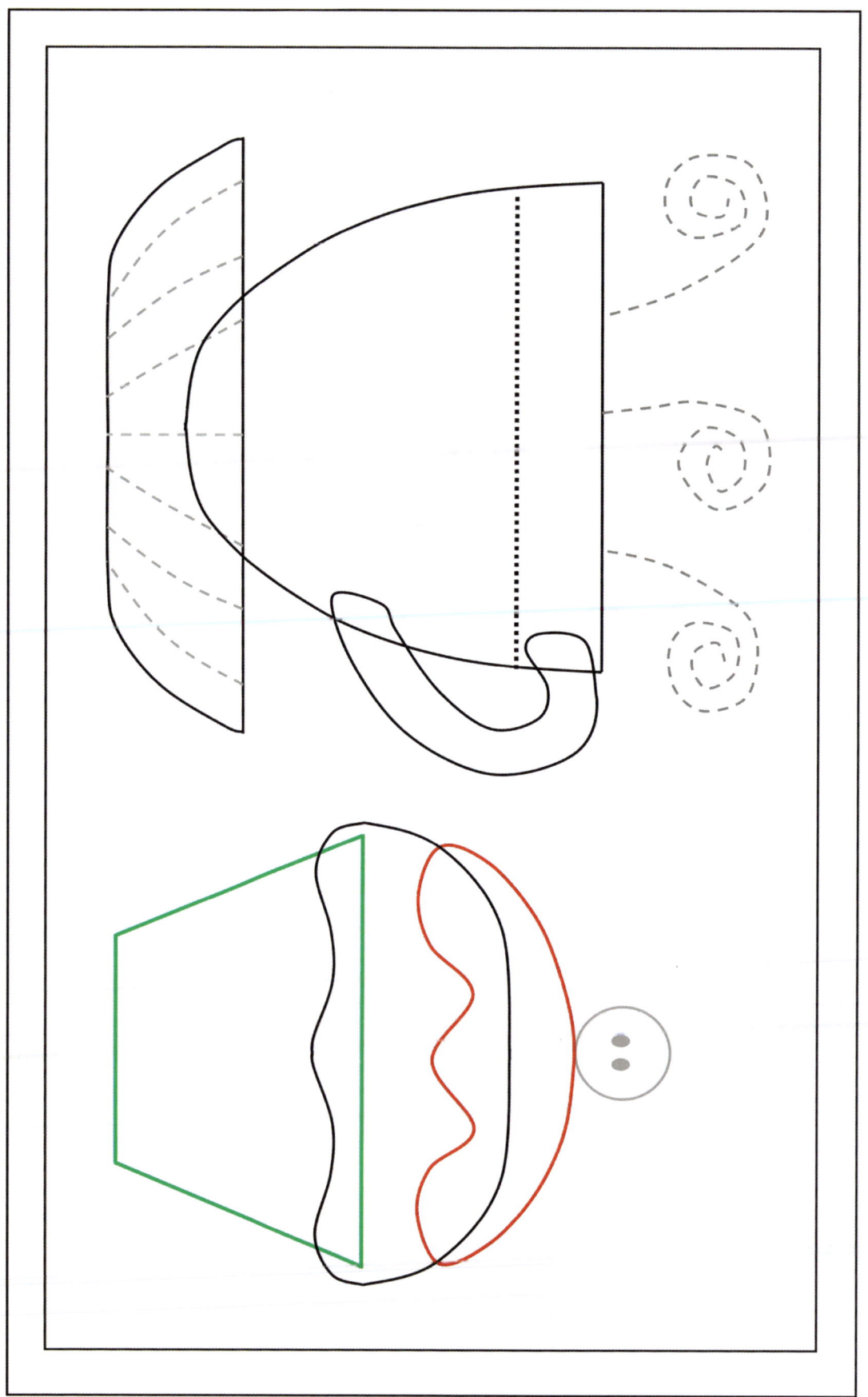

PUMPKIN PATCH MUG RUG
(Finished size: 8½" x 6")

Carve yourself a cheerful spot for your Halloween cuppa
as you add an autumnal touch to your breakfast table or work desk
with this lovely pumpkin mug rug.

Fabric Requirements:

For the small pumpkin:	One 4½" x 4" rectangle
For the large pumpkin:	Three 4½" x 2" rectangles
	(**OR** *one 4½" x 5" rectangle*)
For the stalks:	Two 1" x 1½" rectangles
For the background:	Eight 1½" squares
	Two 1" squares
	Four 2¼" x 1½" rectangles
	One 4½" x 1½" rectangle

One rectangle 10" x 8" cotton fabric for backing
One rectangle 10" x 8" of lightweight batting
1 yard of 1¼" binding fabric (i.e. bias binding or cotton strips)

OPTIONAL: Scraps of fabric, fusible webbing and stranded embroidery thread for the hearts or Halloween faces.

Mug Rug Construction

1. Patch the large pumpkin by stitching the three 4½" x 2" strips together as shown, to create one 4½" x 5" patch. Press the seams open. Use this for the large pumpkin.
Alternatively, you can use one 4½" x 5" rectangle.

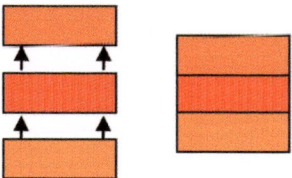

2. Draw a diagonal line in pencil on the back of the 1½" and 1" background squares. This pencil mark will be your stitching line.

3. With RIGHT sides together stitch a 1½" background square onto the top right-hand corner of the small pumpkin 4½" x 4" rectangle as shown. Trim ¼" away from stitched line and press open.

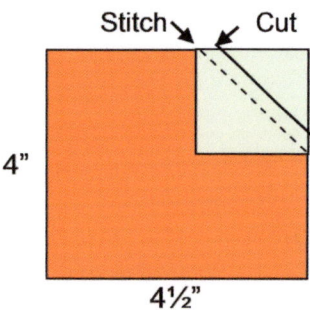

4. Repeat for all corners of both the small and large pumpkin rectangles.

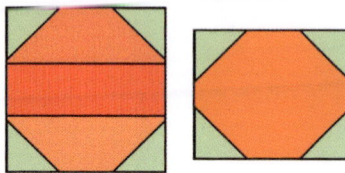

5. With RIGHT sides together place the 1" background squares onto the top of the 1" x 1½" stalk rectangles. (*It doesn't really matter which way you position the diagonal at the top of the stalks*). Stitch along the marked diagonal line, trim and press open as step 3 to create two stalks each measuring 1" x 1½".

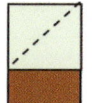 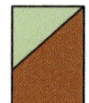 

6. Stitch a 2¼" x 1½" background rectangle to either side of each stalk as shown. Press. The stalk units should measure 4½" x 1½".

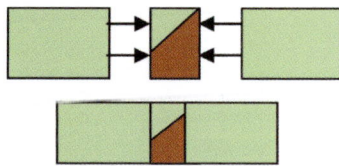

7. Stitch the 4½" x 1½" background rectangle to the top of one of the stalk units to create a small pumpkin top measuring 4½" x 2½". Press the seam towards the top.

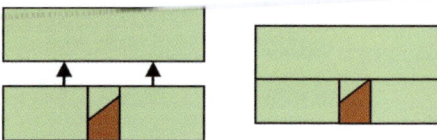

8. With right-sides together, stitch the small pumpkin top to the top of the small pumpkin block and stitch the remaining stalk top unit to the top of the larger pumpkin. Press the seams towards the pumpkins. Both pumpkin blocks should now measure 4½" x 6".

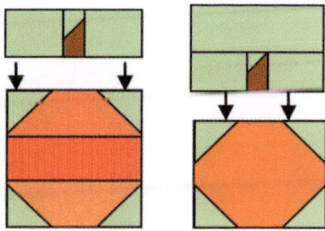

9. Stitch the two pumpkin blocks together as shown to create a mug rug top measuring 8½" x 6". Press.

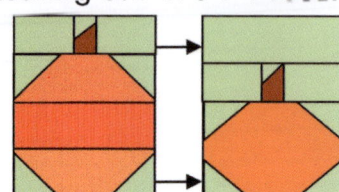

Adding leaves, tendrils and Faces

To add leaves or Jack-O-Lantern faces to your pumpkins, follow the appliqué instructions at the beginning of this book to add your chosen shapes from page 40 to the mug rug.

Note: I added tendrils to the hearts by marking the tendrils with an erasable fabric marker. I then used a simple running stitch and two strands of embroidery thread to stitch over the markings.

Keep it plain and simple for a quick and easy autumnal touch

Completing the Mug Rug

10.   Lay the 10" x 8" backing rectangle, **wrong** side facing up and place the batting on top. Position the appliquéd panel centrally on top with **right** side facing up. Baste or pin all three layers together, ensuring that the backing and top remain flat and smooth. Quilt around each pumpkin. Add pumpkin segment quilting and/or any additional quilting.

11.   Once all quilting has been completed, trim backing and wadding to the same size as the mug rug top.

12.   Bind the mug rug using the binding method of your choice *(see 'Binding' in General Instructions for examples of binding methods).*

PUMPKIN PATCH APPLIQUÉ
*Dashed lines are additional stitching/quilting suggestions as per the pattern.
The Halloween face has been reversed – trace exactly as shown.*

HOLIDAY WREATH MUG RUG
(Finished size: 9" x 9")

Thanksgiving or Christmas – this square mug rug will find a place on any holiday table. Not only will this seasonal wreath support your cup and cookie, it will also provide the perfect resting place for a pie plate or Christmas pudding dish.

Fabric Requirements:

For the Background: One 9 square

For the Wreath: One 7" square

For the Leaves: Ten 3½" squares

For the Bird   One 3" square for the body
Scraps for break, wing and redbreast

You will also need:
One 12" square of fusible webbing (i.e. Bondaweb)
One 11" square of cotton fabric for backing
One 11" square of lightweight batting or fusible batting
1½ yards of 1¼" of binding (i.e. bias binding or cotton strip)

Mug Rug Construction

1. Trace around all appliqué shapes from page 43 onto the paper side of the fusible webbing. Note:
I used ten autumn leaves and eight holly leaves but you may prefer to do more or less.

2. Cut out the shapes roughly - do not cut out accurately along the lines at this stage.

3. Following the manufacturer's instructions, iron the fusible cut-outs onto the WRONG side of your chosen fabric.

4. Allow to cool then cut out the shapes accurately along the traced lines. Peel the paper from each piece.
Tip: If the paper does not come away easily, scratch it carefully with a pin to create a tear. You should then be able to slip the pin between the paper and fabric to separate it.

5. Position the wreath centrally onto the background square. Fuse and stitch the wreath in place.

6. Position the leaves on top of the wreath and the bird in the middle (the beak lies slightly under the bird's body). When happy with the placement iron and stitch in place.

7. Create the bird's eye using two strands of embroidery thread and a small overstitch.

8. Lay the 11" square of backing fabric wrong side facing up and place the batting on top. Position the wreath mug rug centrally on top with **right** side facing up. Baste or pin all three layers together, ensuring that the backing and top remain flat and smooth.

9. Quilt around the wreath, bird and each leaf by hand or machine. Add any additional quilting as desired.
I added veins to each leaf.

10. Once all quilting has been completed, press the mug rug and trim the backing and batting to the same size as the mug rug top.

11. Add small 'berry' Buttons to the Christmas version if desired but ensure it will not cause a cup to topple. If in doubt use a circle of red felt.

12. Bind the mug rug using the binding method of your choice *(see 'Binding' in General Instructions for examples of binding methods).*
I used a single fold binding on both the Autumnal and Christmas mug rugs.

HOLIDAY WREATH APPLIQUÉ

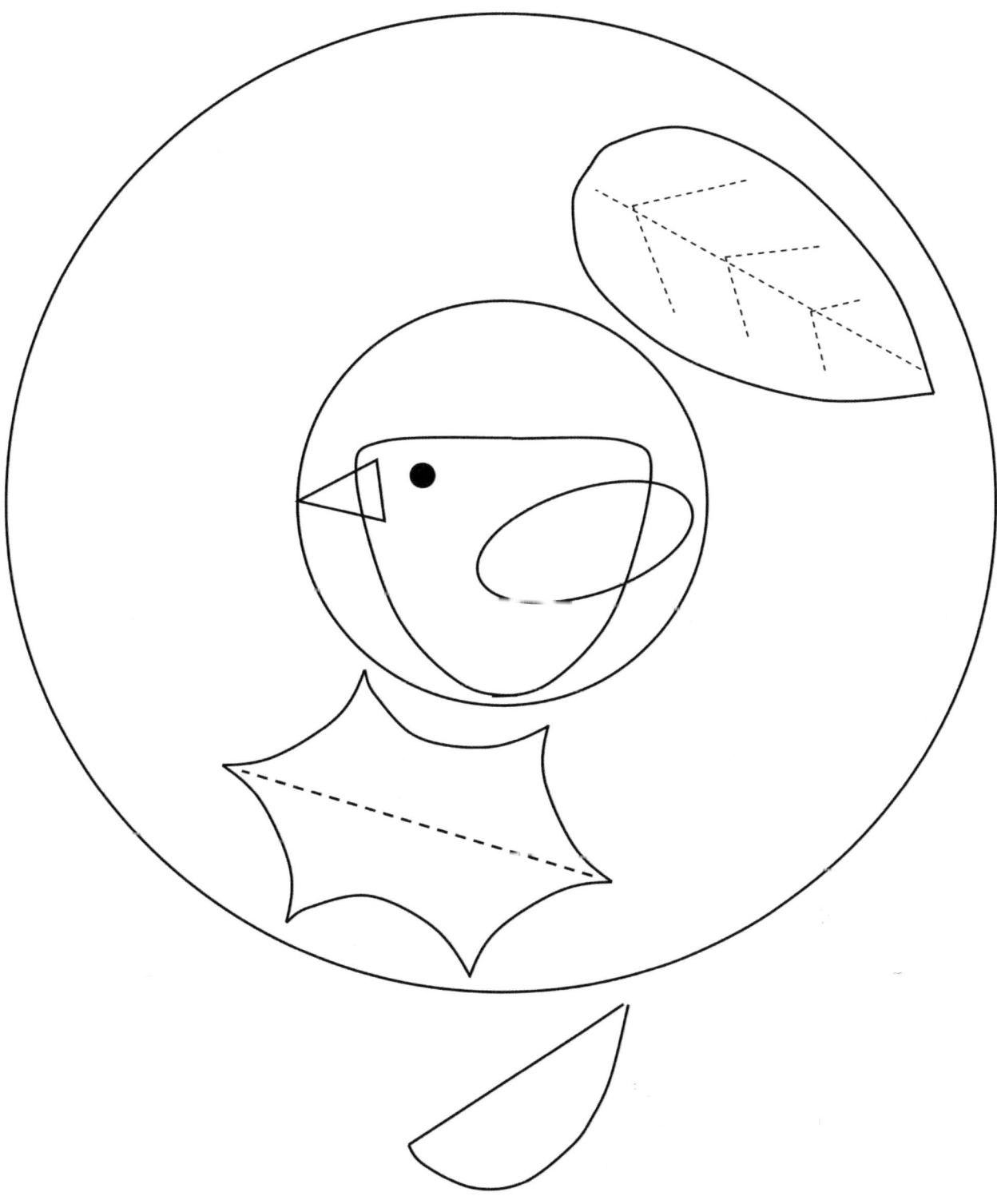

Robin Redbreast
(this image has been reversed - trace exactly as shown)

CHRISTMAS TREE MUG RUG
(Finished size: 7¼" x 9")

No Christmas is complete without a tree or two dotted around the home.
And nothing says 'Merry Christmas' more than a handmade gift.
With this perfectly sized mug rug you can create the perfect place for your
Christmas table or as a special gift for a friend relative or teacher.
And remember – a tree isn't just for Christma

Fabric Requirements:

From tree fabric cut:
(A) Two 2¾" x 2" rectangles
(B) Two 3¼" x 2" rectangles
(C) Two 3¾" x 2" rectangles

From trunk fabric cut:
(D) One ¾" x 5" rectangle

From background fabric cut:
(E) Two 3" x 2¼" rectangles
(F) Two 1½" x 2" rectangles
(G) Two 1" x 2" rectangles
(H) Two 2¼" x 1" rectangles
(I) Two 2½" x 2¼" rectangles
(J) Sixteen 1¼" squares

For the pot cut:
(K) One 3¼" x 2¼" for the pot
(L) One 3¾" x 1" rectangle for the rim

For the top of the tree:
(H) One 2¼" square

See page 50 for the option of appliqueing a star to the top of the tree.

You will also need:
One 8" x 11" rectangle of cotton fabric for backing
One 8" x 11" rectangle of lightweight batting (or heat resistant batting)
1½ yards of 1¼" binding fabric (i.e. bias binding or cotton strip)

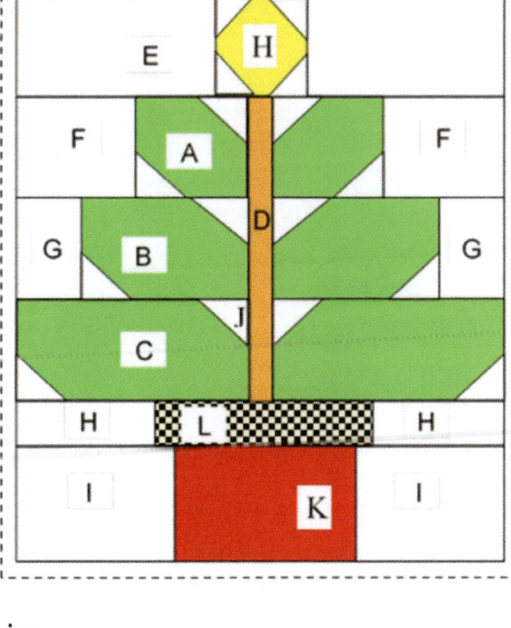

Patching the Tree

1. Draw a diagonal line on the back of all (J) background squares. This line will be your stitching line.

2. With RIGHT sides together place a marked (J) square onto the top right and bottom left corners of one (A) leaf rectangle as shown opposite. Stitch along the marked line. Trim ¼" away from stitched line and press open. Repeat with one (B) and (C) leaf rectangle to create three left-hand leaves for the tree.

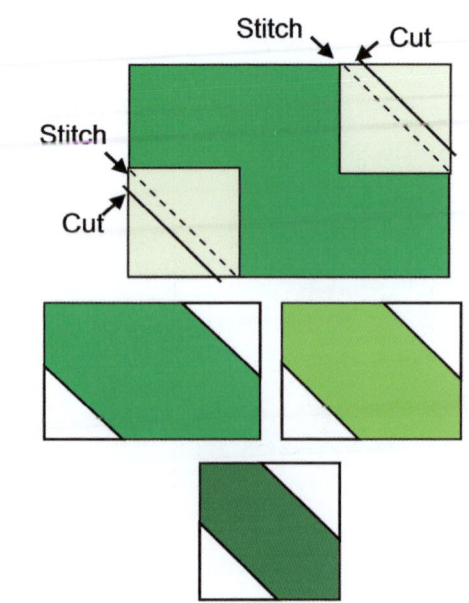

3. With RIGHT sides together place a marked (J) square onto the top left and bottom right corners of the remaining (A) leaf rectangle as shown. Stitch along the marked line. Trim ¼" away from stitched line and press open. Repeat with the remaining (B) and (C) leaf rectangles to create three right-hand leaves for the tree.

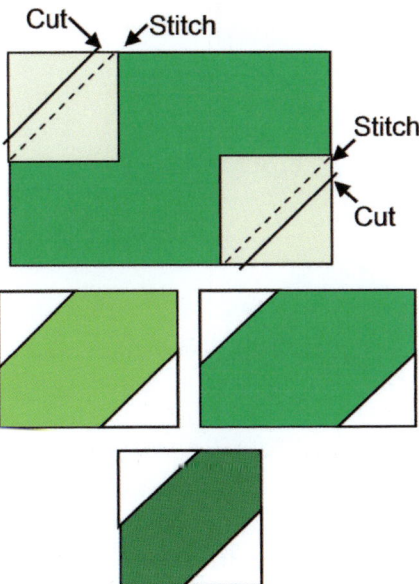

4. With right sides together stitch a (G) background rectangle to the left-hand side of the left B leaf and the right-hand side of the right B leaf as shown below. Press.

5. With right sides together stitch a (F) background rectangle to the left-hand side of the left A leaf and the right-hand side of the right A leaf as shown. Press.

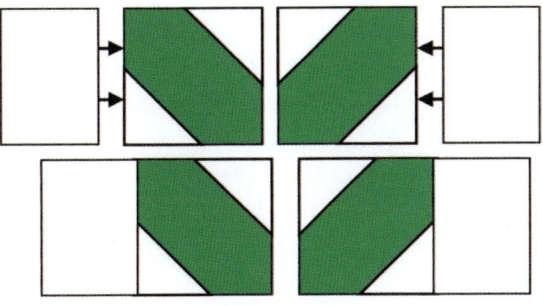

Each leaf unit should measure 3¾" x 2".

6. Stitch the three left-hand leaves together with the (A) leaf at the top and the (C) leaf at the bottom as shown below. Repeat with the three right-hand leaves. Press the seams open to reduce bulk. The leaf units should each measure 3¾" x 5".

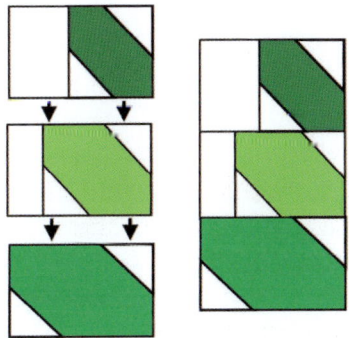

7. With right sides together stitch the left-hand leaf unit to the left side of the (D) trunk rectangle and the right-hand leaf unit to the right side of the (D) trunk rectangle to create a tree measuring 7¼" x 5". Press. (*I pressed the seams towards the trunk so that they overlapped each other but you may prefer to press open or to one side.*)

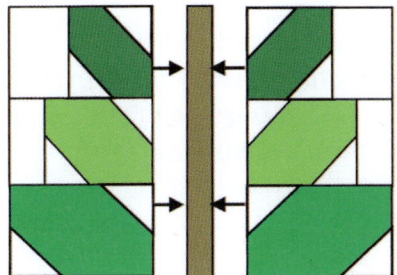

8. Stitch the Two (I) background rectangles to either side of the (K) pot rectangle to create a unit measuring 7¼" x 2¼". Press.

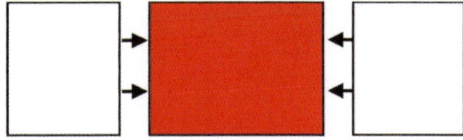

9. Stitch the two (H) background rectangles to either side of the (L) pot rim rectangle to create a unit measuring 7¼" x 1". Press.

10. Stitch the pot rim unit to the top of the pot to create a pot unit measuring 7¼" x 2¾". Press.

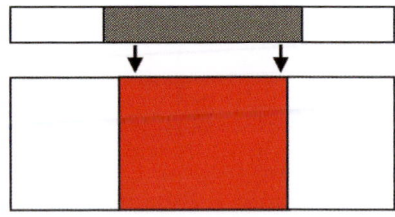

11. Stitch the pot unit to the bottom of the tree to create a unit measuring 7¼" square. Press.

If you are appliquéing a star to the top of your tree go to step S1 below otherwise continue to patch a golden globe for the top of the tree.

12. To create a golden globe for the top of your tree, place a marked (J) background square onto the top right-hand corner of the (H) square, right sides together. Stitch along the marked line, trim and press open as you did when creating the leaves for the tree. Repeat on the other three corners with the remaining (J) squares. The Globe unit should measure 2¼" square.

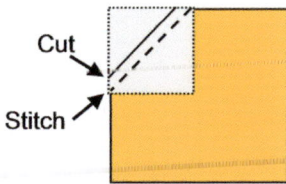

13. Stitch the two (E) background rectangles to either side of the glob unit to create a top tree unit measuring 7¼" x 2¼". Press.

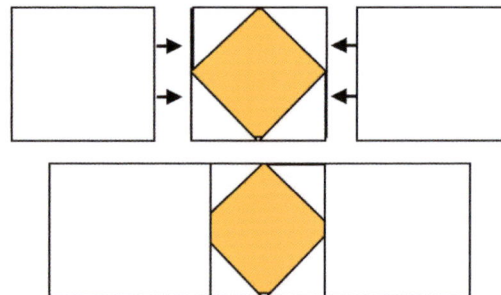

14. Stitch the top tree unit to the top of the tree to create a mug rug measuring 7¼" x 9". Press this seam open. Proceed to step 15 'Finishing the Mug Rug' below.

Star Appliqué
To appliqué a star to the top of the tree you should cut one background rectangle measuring 7¼" x 2¼". You will also need a 4" square of fabric and a 4" square of fusible webbing for the star.

S1.   With right sides together stitch a 7¼" x 2¼" background rectangle to the top of the tree. Press. The mug rug should measure 7¼" x 9".

S2.   Trace around the star shape below onto the paper side of the fusible webbing (Bondaweb). Cut out the traced shape roughly - do not cut out accurately at this stage.

S3.   Following the manufacturer's instructions iron the fusible webbing cut-out onto the WRONG side of your 4" square of fabric.

S4.   Allow to cool then cut out the star accurately along the traced lines. Remove the paper from the back of the star.

S5.   Position the star at the top of the tree ensuring you leave ½" between the top of the star and the edge of the mug rug. When happy with the placement, iron to fuse the star in place. Hand or machine stitch around the star to secure it in place.

Finishing the Mug Rug

15.   Lay the 8" x 11" backing rectangle, **wrong** side facing up and place the batting on top. Position the mug rug centrally on top with **right** side facing up. Baste or pin all three layers together, ensuring that the backing and top remain flat and smooth. Quilt around the tree and globe/star, down either side of the trunk and between each layer of leaves. Quilt around the pot and the pot rim. Add any additional quilting as desired.

16.   Once all quilting has been completed, trim backing and batting to the same size as the mug rug top.

17.   Bind the mug rug using the binding method of your choice *(see 'Binding' in General Instructions for examples of binding methods)*

STAR APPLIQUE

ABOUT THE AUTHOR

I am Amanda Weatherill, also known as the Patchsmith. I live in a little village nestled in the Hampshire countryside where I spend my days designing and making mini quilts - they are my hobby and my passion. My philosophy is simple – share this passion so that everybody has the opportunity to create a little piece of fabric art for their home. Mug rugs are the perfect way to achieve this. Using little more than scraps of fabric you too can enjoy the hobby of mug rug making to create something unique and functional for your desk or table. In so doing you will always have a reminder close to hand of your love of fabric, fun and colour.

Join me as I share my quick and easy designs to help you create a life full of fabric, fun and friends.

You can find the Patchsmith on Amazon, Facebook, Pinterest and Instagram.

To find out more about Patchsmith patterns and mug rug making visit
thepatchsmith.blogspot.co.uk.

Printed in Great Britain
by Amazon